GARVIT

BUGATTI

How did it become the King of Sports Cars?

A BUSINESS CASE STUDY

DISCLAIMER

© 2020 Garvit Yadav

All rights reserved. This book or parts thereof may not be reproduced in any form, stored in any retrieval system, or transmitted in any form by any means- electronic, mechanical, photocopy, recording, or otherwise- without prior written permission of the author, except as provided by United States of America copyright law. The book is based on research from both online and offline sources. The author does not accept any responsibility or liability for the accuracy, content, completeness, legality or reliability of the information contained in the book. The book has been written solely for educational purposes and has not been created with any intent to harm, injure or defame any person, body of persons, association, company or anyone. This book is not intended to spread rumours, offend or hurt the sentiments of any religion, communities or individuals or to bring disrepute to any person (living or dead). The author does not take responsibility for any direct, indirect, implied, punitive, special, incidental or other consequential damages arising directly or indirectly on account of any actions taken based on the book. Readers' discretion is advised.

FOREWORD

Bugatti is one of the few high-end car automakers. It has a distinctive brand image and its car comprises of a blend of advanced engineering and unique artistry. The company's designs are truly artistic which derive inspiration from architectural design and unique sculptures.

Bugatti is a very exclusive brand, a symbol of exotic and luxurious hypercars. Ever since the company was founded, these cars came with a certain passion which is present even today. But, the brand wasn't really full of luck.

Bugatti today is regarded as one of the best supercar manufacturer and has produced many automobile delights since its founding almost 111 years ago in 1909. The company's one of the first cars, the Type 35 Bugatti , is till date regarded as the most race winning car. It is said to have won around 2000 races in its lifetime.

This brand has seen many ups and downs. The period after the death of its founder, Ettore Bugatti was especially difficult for the company .There came a time when it stopped its production due to low sales and huge losses.

Bugatti's success as we see it now, has not been such forever. Overall its rise and fall and the eventual revival by an Italian trader and businessman Romano Artioli is very unique.

In this book we are going to look at the timeline of Bugatti and how it became as it is today. Towards the end we will be looking as Bugatti's functioning as a brand which makes it so special and some of the best cars manufactured by it.

Table of Contents:

PART – 1

   CHAPTER – 1: THE BEGINNING & Success

      Other popular automobiles produced by Bugatti

      Buggati Type 18

      Bugatti Type 29/30

      Bugatti Type 55

      Bugatti Type 57G

      Bugatti Autorail

      Bugatti 100P (Airplane)

   CHAPTER– 2: THE DOWNFALL

PART – 2

   CHAPTER – 3 : ATTEMPTS AT REVIVAL

   CHAPTER – 4 : MODERN REVIVAL

PART – 3

   CHAPTER – 5 : BUGATTI'S RECENT CARS

      Bugatti Veyron 16.4 Grand Sport

      Bugatti 16 C Galibier concept

      Bugatti Veyron 16.4 Super Sport

      Bugatti Veyron 16.4 Grand Sport Vitesse

      Bugatti Chiron

      Bugatti Chiron Sport

      The 100th Chiron

      Bugatti Divo

      Bugatti Chiron Sport '110 ans Bugatti'

      Bugatti La Voiture Noire

      Bugatti Baby II

   CHAPTER – 6: WHY IS BUGATTI SO EXPENSIVE?

      (i) Engine

      (ii) Sound System

PART – 1

The rise and the fall

CHAPTER – 1: THE BEGINNING & Success

Bugatti was founded by an Italian born industrial designer Ettore Bugatti in the year 1909, in the then-German city of Molsheim, Alsace. Ettore was born into an artistic family with his father being an important Italian Art Nouveau furniture and jewelry designer. His paternal grandfather was an architect and sculptor.

It all started in 1898 when Ettore Bugatti was 17-years-old. He made his first vehicle called Type 1. It had four engines (two on each axle), but young Ettore didn't make any more of them. It was just a prototype, which showed Ettore's passion in mechanics. With support from his family, he continued with the idea of making automobiles, and his Type

2 model was presented at the 1901 Milan Trade Fair.

The influence of the artistic family background of Ettore Bugatti can be easily seen in the well designed and mesmerising looks of the initial cars made by him.

The company didn't have the best start due to WWI, but Bugatti survived thanks to making military airplanes. After the war, the production continued in 1919, and the company made 3 new models that would put them on the map. That year, at the Paris Motor Show, the public was introduced to the Type 13, Type 22 and Type 23.

(The Type 13 Bugatti)

(The Type 22 Bugatti)

(The Type 23 Bugatti)

Bugatti saw massive success after the 1919 Paris motor show. The car was an eye catcher and a crowd puller. Bugatti was a real enthusiast car , driven by individuals who were really passionate about automobiles.

The model Type 35 is the most successful racing car of all time, and won more than 2000 races during its time. It even won the legendary Targa Florio race...5 years in a row, and the most famous Type 35 driver was Louis Chiron. Bugatti soon came to symbolize luxury and a wealthy lifestyle not everyone could afford.

Other popular automobiles produced by Bugatti

Buggati Type 18

The Type 18 – nicknamed the 'Black Bess' – was one of the most important Bugattis of the pre-war era and one of the first street-legal race cars. With a top speed of 100mph it was one of the fastest vehicles in the world, which is why it attracted the attention of aviation pioneer, Roland Garros.

He was one of only seven customers for these 5.0-litre, 100hp road rockets. The Type 18 inspired the Bugatti Veyron 16.4 Grand Sport Vitesse 'Black Bess', which was limited to three models, each one with a price tag of €2.15 million.

Bugatti Type 29/30

Although car production ceased during the First World War, the Molsheim factory wasn't left idle. Bugatti developed several airplane engines for the French and American governments, with the proceeds enabling the company to resume automobile production in 1919. Indeed, the number of employees rose to more than 1,000.

In 1921, the Type 28 was built as a prototype, but the large number of patents applied for paved the way for all subsequent Bugatti developments. The following year, Bugatti launched the Type 29/30 (pictured), its first eight-cylinder race car. It achieved a power output of around 80hp and boasted a shape reminiscent of a cigar.

Bugatti Type 55

The beautiful Type 55 was designed by Jean Bugatti and was essentially a touring car with a Grand Prix engine. It used the 2.3-litre supercharged engine from the Type 51 and could be ordered in both two-seat roadster and coupe 'faux cabriolet' forms.

Bugatti Type 57G

And now for something completely different... The 57G 'Tank' was the only Bugatti race car to achieve multiple successes in the latter half of the 1930s, with victories at Le Mans and the French Grand Prix.

At the 1937 Le Mans, Jean-Pierre Wimille set a new lap record speed of 148.98km/h and broke the distance record in the 23rd hour, securing Bugatti's first Le Mans victory in the process. Three 57Gs were built and only one is thought to have survived. In fact, Bugatti's most successful car after its revival, the Bugatti Veyron's body design has been inspired from this car.

Bugatti Autorail

The huge 12.5-litre engine from the Bugatti Royale found an unlikely new home in the form of the Bugatti Autorail of 1932. Bugatti offered to build high-speed train for the French national rail authority in 1931 and won the tender in the face of fierce competition.

Jean Bugatti drove the Autorail on its official test runs at Gallardon, before setting a new record speed of 166km/h on a 24km stretch of track near Le Mans. In 1934, the Autorail achieved a speed of 192km/h over 6km.

Bugatti 100P (Airplane)

<u>Ettore</u> Bugatti started work in 1938 to design a racer to compete in the Deutsch de la Meurthe Cup Race, using engines sold in his automotive line for co-marketing. However, the aircraft never flew as it was not completed by the deadline of September 1939.

The plane was designed by Louis de Monge, a Belgian engineer, who had already applied Bugatti Brescia engines in his Type 7.5 lifting body.

(Bugatti 100P Airplane)

CHAPTER- 2: THE DOWNFALL

Bugatti had seen quick success after the 1919 Paris Motor show by creating a distinct name for itself in the automobile sector. The company also won two Le Mans races (in 1937 and 1939), which increased the reputation to the name and made it one of the most popular brands of its time.

However, Ettore's personal life soon took a downturn which marked the beginning of the company's fall. On 11 August 1939, Ettore Bugatti's son died in a car crash while testing the Type 57 tank bodied race car near the Molsheim factory. It is believed that this is when problems started to hit the company.

In the first months of the World War- II, Bugatti's factory got destroyed. Ettore tried to reconstruct ill but his medical conditions were starting to decline.

In 1947, he died at the age of 65 leaving the company in pieces. Most of the money was split between the families from his two marriages.

In efforts of trying to bring the company back into business his 25-year-old son Ronald, introduced a new car in 1951 , the type 101. Unfortunately, only 6 units of the 101 were made.

The company was also badly hit by the French Horsepower Tax system. This system stated that the bigger the engine in a car, the larger the tax would be. To prevent themselves from paying extra taxes, many people switched to smaller engine cars and Bugatti's had to shut its door in 1952.

PART – 2

ATTEMPTS AT REVIVAL & MODERN REVIVAL

CHAPTER – 3 : ATTEMPTS AT REVIVAL

Under Roland Bugatti, the company attempted a comeback in the 1950s with the launch of the mid – engined Type 251. It was designed by Gioacchino Colombo, an Italian automobile engine designer who had previously worked at Alfa Romeo.

The car failed to gain traction amongst the customers and was unable to perform to expectations. With this, the company's attempts at automobile production were halted. Bugatti continued manufacturing airplane parts.

In the early 1960s, a Bugatti was designed by Virgil Exner as a part of his "Revival Car" projects. A show version of this car was built using the last Bugatti Type 101 chassis by

Ghia and was shown in the 1965 Turin Motor Show. However, as he was unable to get investments to continue working on his project, Exner then turned his attention at reviving Stutz Motor Car company of America.

Bugatti was sold to Hispano – Suiza , a former auto maker turned aircraft supplier , in 1963 for its airplane parts manufacturing business. The company later also acquired Messier in 1968. Bugatti and Messier were merged under Snecma into Messier – Bugatti in the year 1977.

CHAPTER – 4 : MODERN REVIVAL

In 1987 the Bugatti brand was acquired by Romano Artioli, an Italian entrepreneur. He then changed the name and established the brand as we know it today, the Bugatti Automobili S.p.A. Artioli hired an architect, Giampaolo Benedi for designing the factory which was built in in Campogalliano near Modena, Italy.

The construction of the plant began along with the development of the first model in the year 1988. By 1989, the plans for the new Bugatti revival were presented by Paolo Stanzani and Marcello Gandini who had also designed two of the most popular Lamborghinis, the Lamborghini Miura and the Lamborghini Countach.

The first production vehicle was the Bugatti EB110 GT which featured a 3.5 – litre, 5- valve per cylinder, quad – turbocharged 60° V12 engine, a six – speed – gearbox and four – wheel drive. Although, due to a clash between Stanzani and Artioli about the material used for building the body of the chassis , Stanzini left the project.

Artioli sought Nicola Materazzi to replace him in June 1990. Materazzi used a carbon fibre chassis which was manufactured by Aerospatiale and altered the torque distribution of the car from 40:60 to 27:73.

In 1991, exactly 110 years after the birth of Ettore Bugatti, the company was back. The EB 110 was as innovative and evocative as its forebears, boasting a quad-turbocharged V12 engine, permanent four-wheel drive and the world's first carbonfibre chassis.

It also shared something in common with the Type 41 Royale, arriving at a time when the world was plunged into a deep recession. It meant that few people could afford to pay the extravagant price tag.

(The Bugatti EB 110)

By the time the EB110 came to market, the North American and European economies were in recession. Poor economic conditions forced the company to fail and operations ceased in September 1995.

German firm Dauer Racing purchased the EB110 licence and remaining parts stock in 1997 in order to produce five more EB110 SS vehicles. These five SS versions of the EB110 were greatly refined by Dauer. The Campogalliano factory was sold to a furniture-making company, which became defunct prior to moving in, leaving the building unoccupied.

(The Bugatti EB 110 SS)

Predictably, Romano Artioli's vision of a new future for Bugatti failed to materialise and the company was declared bankrupt. But that wasn't before Bugatti was able to build the Super Sport, the ultimate version of the EB 110.

In this guise, the EB 110 SS could achieve a top speed of 195mph, so it's little wonder that Michael Schumacher purchased a yellow car in 1994. He kept it until 2003.

Volkswagen Revives Bugatti

With Bugatti Automobili filing for bankruptcy in 1995, it was left to German sports car manufacturer, Dauer Racing GmbH to pick up the pieces. Production of the EB 110 continued, with a further 10 models completed.

Volkswagen acquired the rights to the brand in 1998 and unveiled the EB 118 in October of that year. The 18-cylinder, Giorgetto Giugiaro-designed four-seat coupe paved the way for one of the most famous cars of the new millennium.

(The Bugatti EB 118)

In 2001, Volkswagen announced that it would be putting a 1,001hp hypercar into production and that manufacturing would take place at Bugatti's rightful home in Alsace. To this end, the company refurbished the traditional company's HQ in Molsheim, calling it 'The Studio'.

Production of the Veyron 16.4 commenced in 2005, with the new Bugatti pushing the boundaries of what was expected from a modern supercar. With a top speed of 400km/h and a 0-62mph time of sub three seconds, the Veyron was a true game-changer.

(The Bugatti Veyron 16.4)

With the launch of the Veyron 16.4 , began the Veyron era which lasted for almost a decade untill 2015. The Veyron's high technological capabilities made it very popular and could be seen in garages of many celebrities and even in videos of songs.

Bugatti was again back in business and would soon dominate the sportscar and the hypercar markets by producing the fastest production car ever. This marked the new era of Bugatti which we now know as the modern era.

PART – 3

Modern Era

CHAPTER – 5 : BUGATTI'S RECENT CARS

Bugatti now had captured a large part of the sportscar marketing thanks to the outstanding marketing and excellent engineering of the Volkswagen group.

Bugatti did not stop after making the fastest production car and continued improving itself and giving many more outstanding and jaw dropping unveils.

Bugatti Veyron 16.4 Grand Sport

In 2008, Bugatti chose the Concours d'Elegance at Pebble Beach to launch the Veyron 16.4 Grand Sport. Chassis number one was sold for $3.2 million.

To mark the centenary of Bugatti in 2009, the company unveiled four 'Centenaire' models, paying tribute to the Type 35. The cars were presented in the colours of the countries that dominated motorsport of the era: blue for France, red for Italy, green for Britain and white for Germany.

(The Bugatti 16.4 Grand Sport)

Bugatti 16 C Galibier concept

Bugatti unveiled the 16 C Galibier concept with a promise to build "the most exclusive, elegant, and powerful four-door automobile in the world". Sounds a little like the Type 41 Royale, then?

It name stems from a complex Alpine pass and a version of the Type 57. Sadly, we're yet to see a modern-day Bugatti four-door.

Bugatti Veyron 16.4 Super Sport

In June 2010, the Bugatti Veyron 16.4 Super Sport broke the speed record for production cars, achieving a top speed of 431.072km/h (267.86mph).

The Super Sport develops 1,200hp and remains the fastest production car on the planet.

Bugatti Veyron 16.4 Grand Sport Vitesse

The Veyron 16.4 Grand Sport Vitesse was unveiled at the 2012 Geneva Motor Show and is essentially an open-top version of the Super Sport. At 408.84km/h (254.04mph) it is the official fastest production roadster in the world.

When news of dieselgate broke, it was thought that development of future Bugatti models might be halted.

(The Bugatti Veyron 16.4 Grand Sport Vitesse)

Bugatti Chiron

At the 2016 Geneva Motor Show, Bugatti unveiled the Chiron: the world's first production car with 1,500hp. "Ready for a new world speed record", said Bugatti when the firm released the performance figures. Even at a base price of €2.4 million, Bugatti had secured advance orders for a third of the total production of 500 units.

In June 2017, Bugatti London welcomed the first Chiron customer car in the UK, painted in the launch colours of the world premiere Chiron. Early in the year, Bugatti announced that half of the total series had already found a buyer – even without test drives.

(The Bugatti Chiron)

Bugatti Chiron Sport

Two years after the launch of the original Chiron, Bugatti followed it up with the Chiron Sport. It retains the 1,500hp powertrain, but Bugatti has developed a dynamic handling package and reduced the weight of the Chiron by 18kg to deliver higher cornering speeds and greater agility.

Even without any extra power, the Chiron Sport can lap the Nardo handling circuit a full five seconds faster than the 'standard' Chiron. The Chiron Sport is distinguished by a new wheel design and four-pipe exhaust deflector, and is the first car to boast carbon fibre windscreen wipers.

(The Bugatti Chiron Sport)

The 100th Chiron

In March 2018, Bugatti celebrated the production and delivery of the 100th Chiron. Its lucky owner opted for a striking combination of dark blue carbon in a matt finish and a red side line. The owner paid a cool €2.85 million (£2.45 million) for the landmark Chiron.

Stephan Winkelmann, Bugatti president, said: "I find the 100th Chiron especially pleasing. It is dynamic and elegant in equal measure. This car shows that Bugatti produces highly individualised masterpieces of automobile craftsmanship that are simply unparalleled.

(The 100th Bugatti Chiron)

Bugatti Divo

Even if you could afford the €5 million (£4.3 million) price tag, you couldn't get your hands on the Bugatti Divo. Not unless you were one of the 40 customers selected by Bugatti. By the time the world got wind of the Divo, each one had already been spoken for.

Again, the power output is the same as the Chiron, but the Divo is 35kg lighter and has 90kg more downforce than its sibling. The result is that this stiffer, lighter, more hardcore and ultra-exclusive Bug' can lap the Nardo circuit eight seconds faster than the Chiron and can hit a top speed of 236mph.

Bugatti Chiron Sport '110 ans Bugatti'

Unveiled in February 2019 and launched to the public at the 2019 Geneva Motor Show, the Chiron Sport '110 ans Bugatti' celebrates 110 years of Bugatti and pays tribute to France.

The French tricolour can be found on the door mirrors, across the fuel filler cap and the underside of the rear wing. The theme continues on the inside, with the French flag embroidered on the headrests, and used to denote the '12 o'clock' mark on the steering wheel.

Bugatti La Voiture Noire

The Bugatti La Voiture Noire pays tribute to the Type 57 SC Atlantic and is the most expensive new car ever built. Once again, the Chiron is the base car, but a long sprawling nose apes the Atlantic, while there are plenty of hints of the track-prepared Divo, too.

At the back, you'll find six exhausts and a distinctive light strip. Only one La Voiture Noire will be built, and the as-yet unknown buyer paid a jaw-dropping £12 million for the privilege of owning the most talked about car at the 2019 Geneva Motor Show.

Bugatti Baby II

Our history ends – and the future begins – with the news that the Bugatti 'Baby' has returned. In 1926, Ettore Bugatti built a toy Type 35 for his youngest son Roland. Such was the response to this one-off design that Ettore was encouraged to put the 'Baby' into production. Around 500 were built and sold between 1927 and 1936.

To celebrate its 110th anniversary, Bugatti has unveiled a tribute to the original, and once again, just 500 will be built. Each one features a rear-wheel-drive battery-powered electric powertrain, removable lithium-ion battery packs, a limited slip differential and regenerative braking. There are two driving modes: 'child', with a top speed of 20km/h; and 'adult', with a top speed of 45km/h. The price: €30,000 (£25,000) plus local taxes.

(The Bugatti Baby II with Bugatti Chiron)

CHAPTER – 6: WHY IS BUGATTI SO EXPENSIVE?

Bugattis are one of the most prestigious cars to own and certainly mark the wealthy lifestyle of the individual. Both of Bugatti's production cars, the Veyron and the Chiron start in seven – figure range.

Other than being super fast, there are many reasons why Bugatti are very expensive.

(i) Engine

The engine used in both of the Bugatti production cars, i.e., the Veyron and the Chiron is a W16 engine. The engine has a displacement of 8.0 L (488 cu in) and four turbochargers.

A W16 engine is a sixteen cylinder piston engine with four banks of four cylinders in a W configuration.

The most powerful version of this engine which is installed in the Bugatti Chiron Super Sport 300+ generates 1578 hp (1177 kW) at 7000 rpm, which is almost double to that of a Lamborghini Aventador.

The engine's rarity also creates a spike in its price as Bugatti's parent company, Volkswagen Group, is the only manufacturer of this engine till now.

Also, there are only 8 technicians who are certified by Bugatti to assemble and make the engine. The engine, which has about 3500 parts is assembled by these technicians.

Once the engine has been assembled, it is put on a test bench, internally developed by the Bugatti's engineers, for 1000 hours.

(ii) Sound System

Each Bugatti produced has a customised sound system which is developed by a specialised and experienced engineer. The sound system does not only include the internal infotainment system but also the external factors which make a drive harmonious.

The Bugatti's sound system also takes into account the sound of the engine and the wind which are also very critical for a good driving experience. The engine's sound needs to comply with the street legal rules while giving the excitement of driving a 1500 horsepower beast.

After the assembling has been complete, an engineer drives the vehicle just to check if all the sound system is working efficiently and harmoniously.

(iii) The Body

Bugattis are one of the fastest production cars and hence, are required to be light in order to gain higher speeds with lesser power. The materials used in a Bugatti are extremely light and Bugatti is willing to pay any price to make a light car.

It uses very expensive and often times the limited edition cars also use very rare materials which might only be seen in F1 cars.

The car chassis are built from aluminium, carbon fiber and titanium which make it very light while also being strong enough to handle the huge forces which act on the car while travelling at very high speeds of almost 200 mph.

The company also tries to make every part of the car as compact as possible so as to fit in a small space.

(iv) Engineering

Each Bugatti car is an engineering marvel. The company tends to ensure each minute detail in order to make the car most efficient and perform its best.

The cars don't have axelled wheels which help the car to gain better grip on the asphalt and prevent the two tonne Bugatti from skidding even while taking a corner on a wet road.

The tires are continuously monitored by a computer. While taking corners, the speed of the outer tires is more than the speed of the inner tires as they tend to cover more distance as compared to the inner tires. At such times, the computer monitors and provides enough power to whichever tire it is required to run smoothly.

(v) Limited Quantity

Bugattis , though very popular, are very limited in number. This rarity also adds up to the price of the Bugattis.

There are supposedly only 500 of each, Veyron and Chiron produced till now all over the world! Yes, not just in America or the Europe, there are just 500 of Veyrons and Chirons on the planet Earth.

The company on average produces about 40 to 50 cars a year. This creates a large demand and supply gap in the market and drives up the price of these cars significantly.

Upcoming Book

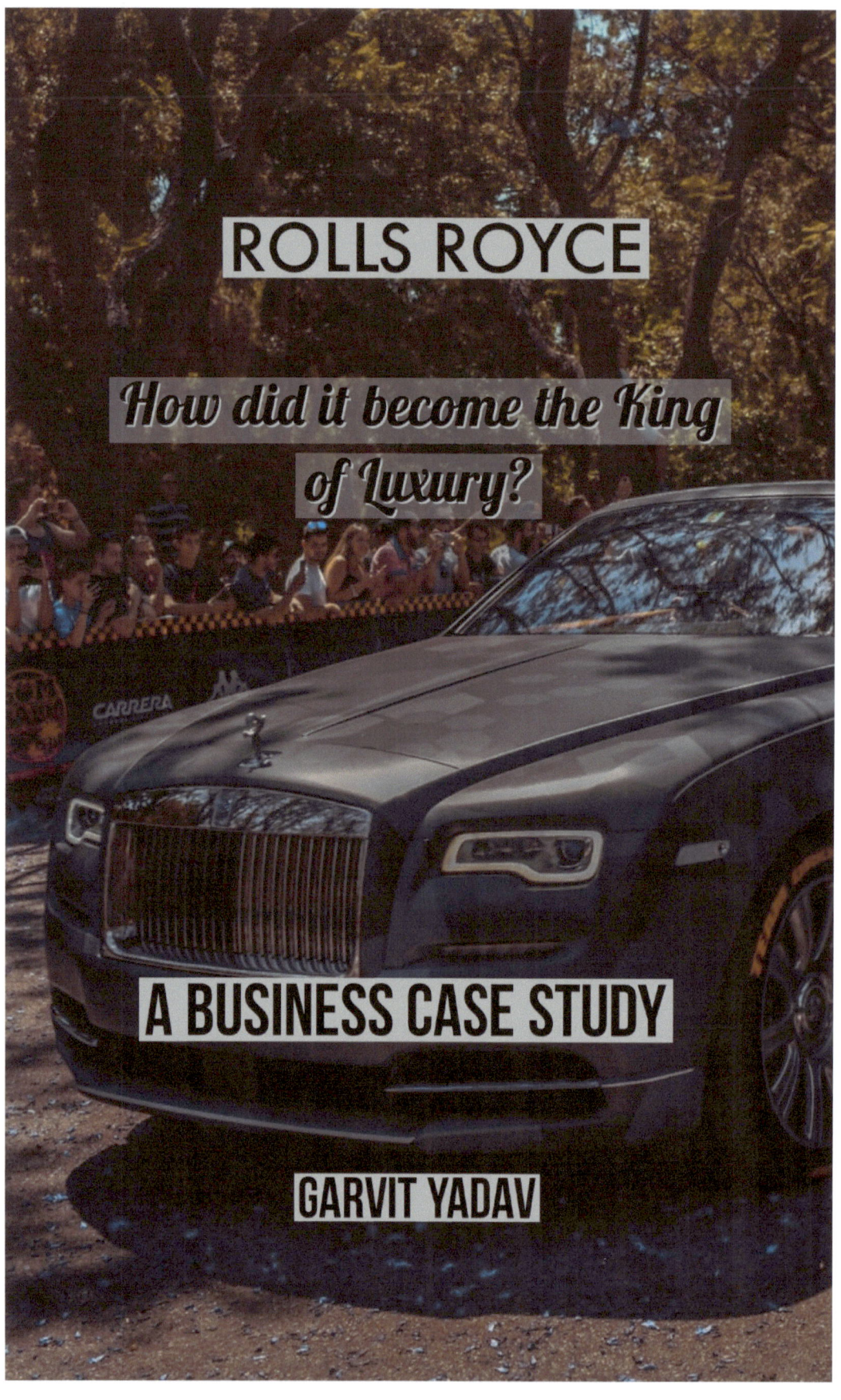